room 1.

BEATRIX POTTER

CHILDREN'S STORYTELLER

BEATRIX POTTER

CHILDREN'S STORYTELLER

By Patricia Dendtler Frevert

Creative Education, Inc.
Mankato, Minnesota 56001

Published by Creative Education, Inc.,
123 South Broad Street, Mankato, Minnesota 56001.

Design: Ned Skubic
Editorial Consultant/Photo Researcher: David Sommer
Cover Design: Susan J. Stavig
Design Consultant: David Jonasson
Editor: Ann Redpath

Photography Credits:
Cover: Frederick Warne & Co., London and New York
Pp. 12, 15, 18, 23, 25, 28, 31: Frederick Warne & Co.,
    London and New York
Pp. 6, 8, 10, 20, 21, 30: George Rodger, LIFE MAGAZINE
    © Time, Inc.
P. 27: Wide World Photos

LIBRARY OF CONGRESS
CATALOG CARD NO.: 80-70966
    Frevert, Patricia
        Beatrix Potter, children's storyteller.
    Mankato, MN: Creative Education
    32 p.
    8103   801211
    ISBN: 0-87191-801-3

For years she invented her own stories of pigs and rabbits, squirrels and ducks. Then, when she was thirty-five years old, she published *The Tale of Peter Rabbit.* Soon others followed: *The Tailor of Gloucester, Squirrel Nutkin, Tom Kitten,* and *Mrs. Tittlemouse* are just a few of the books written and illustrated by Beatrix Potter, a woman who saw the world through the eyes of children. "I used to half-believe and wholly play with fairies when I was a child," she wrote in her secret journal. "What heaven can be more real than to retain the spirit-world of childhood. . . ."

She wrote thirty-one books in all, many of them classics in children's literature. True to her own imagination, Beatrix Potter takes her readers on a journey into "the spirit-world of childhood."

A rabbit, like "Peter Rabbit," outside the garden wall of
Beatrix Potter's farm

*"Now, my dears," said old Mrs. Rabbit one
morning, "you may go into the fields or down
the lane, but don't go into Mr. McGregor's garden:
your father had an accident there; he was put in a
pie by Mrs. McGregor."*

And so the curious Peter, familiar to generations of children everywhere, begins his adventures. By the end of his eventful day, he loses a button, makes a mess of his fine clothes, and nearly ends up as Mr. and Mrs. McGregor's dinner! Happily—and just barely—he returns home safely to Mrs. Rabbit.

Peter and his sisters—Flopsy, Mopsy, and Cottontail—are all inventions of Beatrix Potter. They come complete with clothes, conversation, and problems that blend the animal and human worlds together.

After Peter, many others followed: Squirrel Nutkin, Benjamin Bunny, Mrs. Tiggy-Winkle, Mr. Jeremy Fisher, Tom Kitten, Jemima Puddleduck. They are all an odd mixture of human and animal life as they keep house, take afternoon strolls, and have their friends to tea.

One of Beatrix Potter's watercolors (Other examples of her art are on pages 10, 20, 21, and 27.)

Before he had his own book, Peter Rabbit first appeared in a letter Beatrix Potter wrote to a five-year-old boy.

My Dear Noel,

I don't know what to write to you, so I shall tell you a story about four little rabbits, whose names were Flopsy, Mopsy, Cottontail, and Peter.

The letter went on to tell of bold Peter's adventurous day. In between the handwritten lines were Beatrix's drawings. She drew the mean Mr. McGregor, the garden, and Peter himself—first in his nice new jacket, and then, afterward, exhausted and ragged but finally safe.

It must have been wonderful to receive such a special letter—a letter about a family of rabbits who looked completely real but were carefully dressed in vests and topcoats, taffeta skirts and ribboned bonnets. The animals, small yet serious, were a little like children themselves. Beatrix Potter's letter—weaving its story between fact and fancy—was a treasure to Noel and his brothers and sisters.

London's Bolton Gardens

The letter writer herself—Miss Beatrix Potter of Number Two Bolton Gardens, South Kensington, London—had no idea how special her letter was. Living quietly and almost by herself in her parents' three-story townhouse, she had been drawing and writing for years. In 1893, when she wrote about Peter Rabbit, she was twenty-seven years old.

Sometimes Beatrix sketched Mrs. Tittlemouse nibbling her cheese or caring for her six pink and hairless babies. Occasionally Beatrix drew the snail family that lived in the balcony flower pot. Or the brown bat. Or even the two lizards that sunned themselves each afternoon on the patio tiles.

The isolation in Beatrix Potter's life was not new. From her earliest years she had grown used to the long hours on the third floor of Bolton Gardens. Her window looked out to an elegant urban scene: tall stone townhouses side-by-side, carefully tended gardens, slender boulevard trees. It was a view as ordered and restricted as her life.

Mr. and Mrs. Potter both felt that children needed the company of nurses and governesses rather than parents and other children. Before her brother Bertram was born, Beatrix's only company was Nurse McKensie. Over the years, young Beatrix discovered other companions. She began collecting pets—not just ordinary dogs and cats, but more unusual animals as well. She started her collection at the age of six, with a solitary mouse she called "Hunca Munca." When she

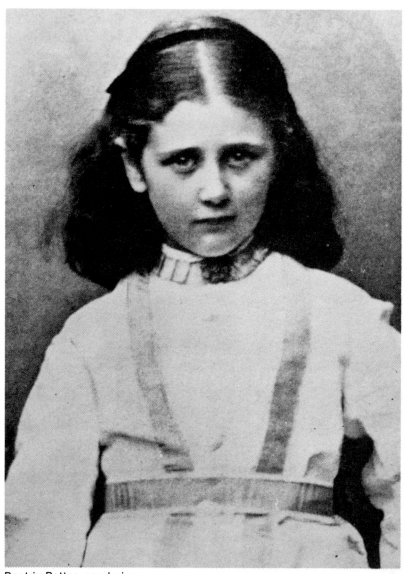

Beatrix Potter, aged nine

found Hunca a wife, named "Appley," a family of mice soon followed. Beatrix hid them in a secret box near her own bed.

Once Bertram was old enough, he began to share his sister's affection for animals. Hunca and Appley were grandparents and then great-grandparents. Together Beatrix and Bertram named and cared for each new generation. By this time, the Potters couldn't help noticing the small zoo that occupied Bolton Garden's third floor. But they didn't interfere.

When Beatrix was nine years old, the year was 1875. Wealthy families observed certain Victorian customs. Women stayed at home doing needlework, entertaining their friends, and pursuing cultural interests. Infants and little children belonged in the nursery, while boys went to school and girls were taught at home by governesses.

Beatrix Potter's parents were proud of the fact that they didn't have to work. Rupert Potter had inherited the fortune his parents had made in the textile industry. He spent some of his time studying photography.

Beatrix and Bertram had a daily routine. They were awakened every morning at seven. Nurse McKensie dressed Bertram and lit a coal fire. At eight o'clock a maid brought breakfast to the nursery. From nine to twelve Beatrix had lessons with Miss Hammond, her governess.

When the lessons were over, the maid served their lunch—often a cutlet and a rice pudding. In the afternoon, McKensie took Bertram walking in the park. Although the Potters objected, Miss Hammond often took Beatrix on long, unplanned walks.

Miss Hammond had arrived when Beatrix was only five years old, right after Bertram was born. The governess quickly noticed her student's observant eye. One day Miss Hammond pointed to some mushrooms that grew in a circle and explained that the Irish called this circling "Fairy Rings." Beatrix was immediately fascinated. She later returned to the mushrooms and brought along a paper and pencil so that she could draw them. Miss Hammond saw that the careful drawing was amazingly accurate.

Soon, with her governess's encouragement, young Beatrix was drawing whatever they collected from their daily walks—foxgloves, Canterbury bells, even bramble leaves. Finally Miss Hammond gave Beatrix a paintbox. Now she could do her work in color.

Beatrix wanted to learn about anatomy so that she could draw animals more accurately. Unlike flowers and mushrooms, live animals squirmed and wiggled and refused to sit still. No matter how hard she tried, she couldn't quite draw them realistically. Miss Hammond figured out a way to solve this problem. She suggested they visit the Kensington Museum. There the butterflies were under glass, and the stuffed owls—perched silently and staring straight ahead—were perfect subjects for Beatrix to study.

Visits to the museum became part of Beatrix's daily routine, and she learned to draw animals as well as plants. Between her live pets at home and the collections at the museum, she spent most of her free time with animals.

One summer when Miss Hammond returned to her own

Beatrix Potter, aged ten

family, she left Beatrix a long note about the months ahead:
Somehow, get yourself over to Kensington Museum as often as possible. I've written Miss Woodward to expect you. I'm about to write to your parents too, and McKensie. There is no reason why McKensie can't trundle Bertram over to the Museum.... Of course, you are seven years old and now ought to be allowed to take that short walk by yourself. I'd write and suggest this to your parents, if I thought it would do any good. But just getting there is what's important, because you've already learned to teach yourself....

Although they hesitated at first, her parents soon consented to the museum visits.

Late in the summer, the family took its annual vacation to the Scottish countryside. The generous rural landscape was a wonderful change for Beatrix, who was used to the confined view from the third floor of Bolton Gardens.

Everything in the country was new and exciting. Beatrix and Bertram explored constantly. They roamed down country lanes and peeped over stone walls. They captured toads and woodmice, built them homes, and gave them each a name.

As Beatrix wandered through the flowered meadows, she easily imagined a fairyland among the wildflowers. She could picture tiny creatures hiding under mosses and mushrooms. Suddenly Beatrix wanted to paint everything she saw. All the cottages had colorful gardens. She drew yellow snapdragons, blue larkspurs, and pink foxgloves. She sketched the farm animals and the soft rolling hills.

A New Friend

When Beatrix was twelve, the Potters planned a vacation in England's Lake District. Packing up the frogs, blue jays, and whatever else the children had collected, they left London for Wray Castle, near Lake Windermere. The new vacation spot turned out to be important to Beatrix, for this was the neighborhood of Canon Rawnsley, the Vicar of Wray.

Dressed in black and wearing a high, stiff collar, the Canon seemed a little frightening at first. But his knowledge of plants and animals soon made Canon Rawnsley so interesting that twelve-year-old Beatrix began to look forward to his company. On long walks together, they collected mushrooms which she could later identify and catalog. By the time she returned to Bolton Gardens that fall, Beatrix was sure she had found a new friend. She was right. In later years, the Canon would help Beatrix make an important decision.

After a summer of outdoor freedom, the third floor of her parents' townhouse was a small gray world. Taking the Canon's advice, Beatrix began a diary.

Toby, our lizard, died today. I think he was very old. He was so stiff and had lost so many toes…. I went to the dentist for the first time in my life. He filled a little hole in one of my upper teeth. It was much simpler than I expected. He did not hurt me at all….

She missed her new friend, but the diary gave Beatrix someone to talk to. And, for reasons that she kept to herself,

Beatrix Potter, aged sixteen

Beatrix wanted the diary to be a secret. She developed a code so nobody else could read what she wrote. It wasn't until after her death that a biographer finally figured out the secret alphabet and was able to read what young Beatrix had carefully and privately written. Beatrix kept her diary for fifteen years—until she had finally found another, more public way, to express herself.

As she grew into womanhood, her habits of isolation didn't change. People began to call her "old-fashioned," and "strange." Unlike the typical Victorian young woman of her background, she did not marry or socialize with other people her age. Instead, she preferred to direct her energy toward her animals, her secret writing, and her art.

Bertram, also interested in art, took off for Scotland and declared himself a painter. Though his parents were confused by this, they did not stand in his way. Beatrix, not yet sure what she wanted, stayed home.

Whenever she showed her drawings to others—especially Canon Rawnsley—they encouraged her to try to find a publisher for them. Hesitant at first, she finally illustrated some greeting cards and a book of someone else's poetry. She had still not discovered that she could put her own art and language together.

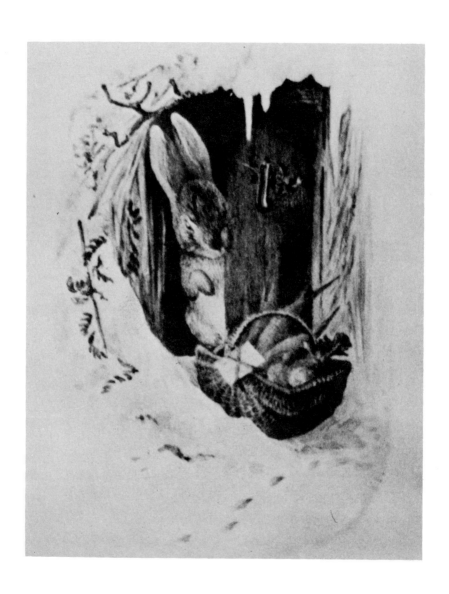

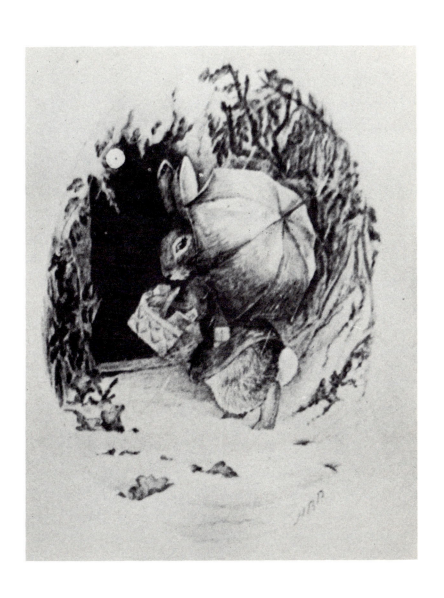

The Letter to Noel

Beatrix had a friend, Annie Moore, who had once been her tutor and was now raising a family of her own. The Moores lived in London, not far from Bolton Gardens, and Beatrix often drove her pony carriage to their home to visit. Sometimes she brought along her cage of white mice and invented mice stories to entertain the children.

The Moore youngsters loved these visits. They didn't know many grown-ups who cared for mice or told long, imaginary stories about how a typical mouse-family might spend its day.

Then one afternoon in 1893 Beatrix got a letter from Annie Moore, who was worried about her oldest child. "Noel is very ill," she wrote. "The doctor says he'll have to stay in bed for quite a while." Beatrix read on.

Can you imagine a five year old being tied down to his bed? He's been good about it so far... but I know we can't continue this pace of keeping him occupied. Besides killing us, it might turn Noel into a spoiled and demanding little boy.... He'll have to learn to entertain himself.

Not knowing how else to help, and unable to visit, Beatrix wrote Noel the letter that would later be famous. "My dear Noel," she began, "I don't know what to write to you, so I shall tell you a story about four little rabbits. . . . "

Six months later, Beatrix wrote to Noel's brother, Eric,

Beatrix Potter, aged thirty

about a pig who lived with some sailors on a ship and was worried about ending up as someone's dinner. This resourceful pig escaped, went to live on Robinson Crusoe's island, and became known as Little Pig Robinson.

In another letter, Beatrix wrote about a squirrel who had no tail. She named him Squirrel Nutkin, and she drew squirrels who paddled across a lake on rafts, using their tails for sails.

The Moore children treasured all her letters. Their mother tied them into a bundle with yellow ribbon and put them away for safekeeping. As the letters collected dust in the attic, Beatrix herself continued to search for the right work. She wrote a scientific paper on mushrooms, and she began to study photography.

But something was wrong. When she visited her brother on his farm in Scotland, she realized that she envied his independence, his sense of knowing what he wanted.

Canon Rawsley, now her friend of many years, was watching Beatrix closely. He thought her drawings of mushrooms were some of the best he'd ever seen, and he was a fairly good botanist himself. He urged her to become a scientific illustrator, but she was unwilling to get the extra training that would require.

Then one day Beatrix hesitantly described her funny little stories about animals who talked and wore clothes. The Canon listened carefully and then suggested that she put one of her stories into a book and start looking for a publisher.

But the stories were all in letters, Beatrix had to explain.

And the letters were mailed to the Moore children long ago—she wasn't even sure they still existed.

"Well, find out!" the Canon insisted. And when Beatrix inquired, she discovered, of course, that the well-loved letters were safe and intact.

Beatrix with her brother Bertram and the family dog

Peter Rabbit: A Book At Last

Beatrix carefully copied the words and pictures from Noel's letter onto fresh pages and added a few new ideas here and there. One month after talking to the Canon, she sent *The Tale of Peter Rabbit* to seven publishers.

Within weeks, all seven publishers turned her down. Having come this far, though, Beatrix was not ready to give up. She decided to publish *Peter Rabbit* herself. She took money out of her savings account, gathered the pages of her book together, and went in search of a printer.

In 1901 she received 250 copies of *The Tale of Peter Rabbit*. The tiny books, measuring about five inches by four inches, sold for one shilling and two pence each and were soon gone. Then Frederick Warne & Company, one of the publishers who had turned her down only months earlier, took another look at *Peter Rabbit* and decided to publish it.

Success made Beatrix bolder. She agreed to let Warne publish her book, and in the meantime she published a second one, *The Tailor of Gloucester*. She was now thirty-six years old.

The little books sold very well. It didn't take long before Warne & Company realized the value of their new author. They encouraged Beatrix to turn all of her old letters into stories and invent new ones.

For the next twelve years, Beatrix Potter did just that. Children everywhere got to know Hunca Munca, Mrs. Tiggy-Winkle, and all the others. As she became famous, the

Beatrix with her husband William Heelis

sheltered Victorian life of Beatrix Potter gradually began to change.

Her work with Warne & Company required that she visit the publishing office regularly. When, in 1905, Beatrix announced that she intended to marry one of the publisher's sons, Norman Warne, her parents were offended and refused to give their consent.

Norman Warne, they insisted, was not their social equal—he was from a family of tradespeople. But Beatrix, who had found mostly sadness and solitude in her own leisure-class childhood, did not consider Norman's social station an obstacle. She wanted to marry him anyway.

The matter was never resolved. Norman, whose health always had been poor, died later that same year—before any marriage could take place.

Still determined to find a life of her own, Beatrix bought a farm in Sawrey—in the Scottish countryside she had grown to love during so many childhood summers. Then, in 1913, she married William Heelis, the lawyer who had helped her purchase the farm she now called Hill Top. She was forty-seven years old.

By the time she married, Beatrix Potter had written and illustrated over twenty books. The picture-letters to the Moore children had become a small library.

As she grew old, she settled into country life. She devoted herself to caring for her land and animals. For a while she tried to continue writing—so many people asked her to. Finally she stopped.

Sometimes she grew tired of her popularity and all the demands for more books. But children were really her first love. She wrote right to their hearts—with the detail, accuracy, and magic that makes a children's story come alive.

By the time she died in 1943, Beatrix Potter's books were already in the dreams of three generations of children. And today, nearly fifty years later, Peter Rabbit and his friends wait—well-worn and loved—in children's libraries everywhere.

A view of Beatrix Potter's Hill Top Farm

31